You Are a Powerful Creator, My Little One

Creating Happiness

Written by Monica Iglesias
Illustrated by Robert Paul Matheus

From My Heart to Yours!

Based on actual events

Copyright © 2014 Monica Iglesias.

All rights reserved. No part of this book may be used or reproduced by any means, graphic, electronic, or mechanical, including photocopying, recording, taping or by any information storage retrieval system without the written permission of the publisher except in the case of brief quotations embodied in critical articles and reviews.

Balboa Press books may be ordered through booksellers or by contacting:

Balboa Press
A Division of Hay House
1663 Liberty Drive
Bloomington, IN 47403
www.balboapress.com
1 (877) 407-4847

Because of the dynamic nature of the Internet, any web addresses or links contained in this book may have changed since publication and may no longer be valid. The views expressed in this work are solely those of the author and do not necessarily reflect the views of the publisher, and the publisher hereby disclaims any responsibility for them.

Any people depicted in stock imagery provided by Thinkstock are models, and such images are being used for illustrative purposes only.
Certain stock imagery © Thinkstock.

ISBN: 978-1-4525-1587-8 (sc)
ISBN: 978-1-4525-9856-7 (hc)
ISBN: 978-1-4525-1588-5 (e)

Printed in the United States of America.

Balboa Press rev. date: 11/18/2014

BALBOA
PRESS
A DIVISION OF HAY HOUSE

DEDICATION

This book is dedicated to my children, especially Francesco who embraces the powerful creator he is and is stepping up to be a positive influence in the world. I am honored to be called his mother.

ACKNOWLEDGEMENTS

I would like to express my sincerest gratitude . . .

❤To God, the angels, and my mother for supporting, guiding, inspiring, and loving me throughout my life and all of its challenges, and for assisting this work to move forward from beyond the veil.

❤To Frank, my husband, best friend, lover, and "Mr. Perfect for me," for loving me unconditionally and allowing me to BE who I was created to be. I love you so much!

❤To the Impact Trainings and their amazing staff for providing the environment that has assisted me in awakening to the powerful creator that I AM.

❤To all whom I had perceived as abusers in my life. Forgive me for the judgments and blame I had placed on you. I am truly grateful for the role you have played in my life. Thank you for showing up in such a way that I could experience myself as who I am.

I honor each of you.

Thank you! Thank You!! THANK YOU!!!

HOW THIS BOOK CAME TO BE

I always wanted to have an open relationship with my children, especially in their teenage years. I knew that in order for that to happen, I needed to start developing that relationship at a young age. But I struggled, as many young mothers do, with maintaining my sanity while juggling three young children.

Having been raised in difficult and what many would perceive as abusive circumstances, I had the tendency to be harsh, impatient, controlling and overbearing with my children, especially my oldest son, Francesco. But I saw what my actions - or should I say "reactions"- were doing to him and I didn't like the results. I knew there had to be another way. I knew that *I* had to change. After pouring out my soul to my Creator, I found myself in a training that assisted me in waking up to the power within me. As I took accountability for what I had experienced in my life, I forgave those whom I had perceived as abusers and was able to move on, choosing to create a better life for myself. This opened up a freedom inside of me that I had never experienced before. I was no longer a victim of my circumstances. I had awakened to a power within myself and it was beautiful to me. In turn, I wanted to share this with my children. As I did, they grasped the concept quickly. I found that when I asked a few simple questions and trusted fully that they had the answers within them, I was fascinated by what they were able to create.

Today, we co-create a beautiful relationship: one of love, peace, joy and mutual admiration. We still have issues that come up, as everyone does, but we are able to move past them quickly and create wonderful results.

This book is the first in a series that portrays amazing things that can be consciously created – all of which my children have inspired through their own actions. There is no accident that you were drawn to this book and chose to pick it up and read it, whether for a child, student, or for yourself. There are powerful truths evident within. As you read this book, although it is written in the form of a children's book, ask yourself the questions within the story, go within your soul / spirit for the answers, and have the courage to act upon the answers you receive.

May God and the Angels assist you in your efforts to create a beautiful life for yourself and those around you, and may your positive influence be felt throughout the world.

One summer morning, mother invited her son, Francesco, to sit on her lap. She was waking up to the powerful creator she was and was excited to share this awareness with her son.

"Do you know that you are a powerful creator, my little one?" mother began. "For good or bad, positive or negative, we create the world around us. We are children of a divine, powerful Creator, and because we are His children, we are also powerful creators.

"There are many things we can create, but not just things with our hands. We can also create happiness, joy, love, acceptance, and even sadness, anger, fear and distrust." Francesco listened intently, absorbing this new information.

"So what do you choose to create today?" his mother asked.

"I want to create HAPPINESS!" He responded with a smile.

"So you *choose* to create happiness?" mother clarified.

He nodded his head with excitement.

"What are some ways you can create happiness?" his mother inquired.

"I can share with my brother and sister . . . I can be nice to them . . . I can do funny things to make them laugh . . . I can help you . . ." The ideas on how to create happiness kept flowing to him.

"Excellent!" mother said, "Those are all wonderful ways to create happiness . . . and do you know where happiness starts?"

Francesco looked at his mother curiously. Then she placed her hand on his heart.

"It starts right here," she said, "with a feeling in your heart. Then it sparks good thoughts in your mind, lights up your face, and trickles out through your actions."

His posture transformed as he listened. He sat up straight and tall, shoulders back, and a smile lit up his face. Watching this transformation, his mother knew he had understood every word she said.

"Now that you know where happiness starts," she continued, "go and create it."

Francesco jumped down off his mother's lap, and with a spring in his step, a smile on his face, and a happy feeling in his heart, he set out to create happiness that day. He did a wonderful job of creating it all morning.

He helped his mother with the dishes.

He was nice to his baby sister.

He played with his brother and sister, and he even did funny

things to make them laugh . . .

all the while being happy in his heart.

Later in the afternoon, Francesco and his little brother, André, were playing cars outside with their friends. André loved cars and really wanted to play with Francesco's car, but Francesco kept telling him to "wait" and wasn't giving him a turn.

André felt
sad
and
left out.

He turned and
silently
walked
away
with his
head
down
low.

He entered the house and walked
past his mother to his bedroom.

Mother noticed André walking by and knew exactly what had happened, having observed the boys through the doorway.

She called out to Francesco as a loving reminder, "Francesco, what did you choose to create today?"

"HAPPINESS!" he exclaimed as he stood up tall, shoulders back, with a big smile on his face.

"Is that happiness just for you?" mother inquired.

Immediately his expression changed to concern as he looked around and realized he had forgotten about his brother.

"Is my brother sad?" he asked.

"You might want to check that out," mother replied in a gentle, loving voice.

He ran to the bedroom and discovered that his brother was feeling sad and left out. Francesco happily invited his brother to rejoin the group and handed him his car.

"Here, you can play with my car," Francesco told André as they walked back outside.

Later that evening, mother called Francesco to sit with her once again. She lifted him up onto her lap.

"So, what did you choose to create today?" mother inquired once more.

"Happiness!" he exclaimed as he sat up tall with a big smile on his face as he had many times that day.

"Well . . . *did* you create happiness?" mother asked.

"Yes, I did!" he said with confidence. "I helped you with the dishes, I was nice to my sister, and I even shared with André."

"Yes, you did!" mother agreed. "There was a moment when there was something other than happiness," mother reminded him, "but you did a wonderful job of shifting even that and created happiness once again! Look what a powerful creator you are!"

Francesco felt that truth in his heart.

"There are so many more things you can create,"
mother added. "Perhaps tomorrow you will choose
to create something new, or you may even choose to
create happiness again."

"But more importantly . . .

Where does happiness start?"

"It starts in my heart!"

Sometimes we create the following unconsciously (without being aware). These feelings are heavy and usually not very pleasant to experience. But at any moment we become aware that these are our results, we have the power to shift and create something different, simply by asking ourselves the questions in this book and acting on the answers we receive.

sadness	fear
anger	shame
resentment	loneliness
guilt	envy
pity	distrust
blame	jealousy
sorrow	frustration
despair	pessimism
depression	worry

Below are some possibilities that you, your child(ren), student(s), or client(s) may choose to create. You may want to introduce these concepts a few at a time and explain what they mean.* Then ask them what they "choose" to create and how they would go about creating it. When they create what they set out to, it is important to celebrate the Powerful Creator they are.

Love	Connection	Accountability
Peace	Unity	Integrity
Happiness	Health	Friendship
Joy	Abundance	Honor
Trust	Compassion	Acceptance
Strength	Gratitude	Equality
Power	Serenity	Freedom
Beauty	Inspiration	Empowerment
Light	Passion for life	Creativity
Transformation	Win/wins	Enthusiasm
Forgiveness	Courage	Celebration

* Whereas connotations of words may change over time, you may want to look up the word definitions in a dictionary.

CPSIA information can be obtained at www.ICGtesting.com
Printed in the USA
BVOW11s2017040115

381774BV00002B/8/P